FROM TADPOLE TO FROG

Anita Ganeri

Heinemann Library

Chicago, Illinois

Customer Service 888-454-2279
Visit our website at www.heinemannraintree.com

Designed by Ron Kamen and edesign
Printed and bound in China by South China Printing Company

10 09 08 07 06
10 9 8 7 6 5 4 3 2 1

Library of Congress Cataloging-in-Publication Data
Ganeri, Anita, 1961-
  From tadpole to frog / Anita Ganeri.
     p. cm. -- (How living things grow)
  Includes bibliographical references.
  ISBN 1-4034-7859-7 (library binding - hardcover) -- ISBN 1-4034-7868-6 (pbk.)
  1. Frogs--Life cycles--Juvenile literature. 2. Tadpoles--Juvenile literature. I. Title. II. Series.
  QL668.E2G35 2006
  597.8'9--dc22
                                2005026923

Acknowledgments
The author and publishers are grateful to the following for permission to reproduce copyright material: Alamy p. **26**;
Ardea p. **5**; Bruce Coleman p. **20** (Kim Taylor); Corbis pp. **6** (Anthony Cooper/Ecoscene), **8** (Jean Hall/Cordaiy Photo
Library Ltd); FLPA pp. **9** (Wil Meinderts/Foto Natura), **11** (Alwyn J. Roberts), **21** (Walter Rohdich), **22** (Derek
Middleton), **23** (Rene Krekels/Foto Natura), **29** (John Tinning); Naturepl.com pp. **4** (William Osborn), **7** (Philippe
Clement), **15** (Jurgen Freund); NHPA pp. **16** (Trevor McDonald), **17** (Stephen Dalton), **19** (Stephen Dalton), **24** (George
Bernard), **25** (Stephen Dalton); Photolibrary.com pp. **10**, **12**, **13**, **14**, **27**; Science Photo Library p. **18** (Dr. Morley Read).

Cover photograph of a frog reproduced with permission of Corbis/Mary Ann McDonald.

Illustrations by Martin Sanders.

Every effort has been made to contact copyright holders of any material reproduced in this book. Any omissions will be
rectified in subsequent printings if notice is given to the publisher.

The paper used to print this book comes from sustainable resources.

Some words are shown in bold, **like this**. You can find out
what they mean by looking in the glossary.

Contents

Have You Ever Seen a Frog?

A frog is a kind of animal called an **amphibian**. They spend part of their lives in water and part on land. Frogs live all over the world.

This is a frog called a common frog.

Frogs spend most of their time in water.

You are going to learn about a common frog. You will learn how a frog is born, grows up, has babies, gets old, and dies. This is the frog's life cycle.

How does the frog's life cycle start?

Laying Eggs

The frog starts life as a tiny egg in a pond. A **female** frog lays the eggs in the spring. The batch of eggs is called a **clutch**.

The female lays hundreds of eggs at a time.

The eggs are covered in clear jelly. The jelly swells up in the water. This helps to keep the eggs safe.

The eggs stick together in a big ball.

What is in an egg?

Hatching Eggs

Can you see the little black animal in each egg? Each one is a tadpole. The tadpole grows bigger and bigger in the egg.

This tiny tadpole will grow into a frog.

The eggs start to **hatch** after about 30 days. The tadpoles wriggle out of their jelly eggs.

Lots of eggs and tadpoles are eaten by fish and birds.

Does the tadpole look like a frog?

9

Tiny Tadpoles

The tadpole does not look like an adult frog. The tadpole has a long tail that she uses for swimming.

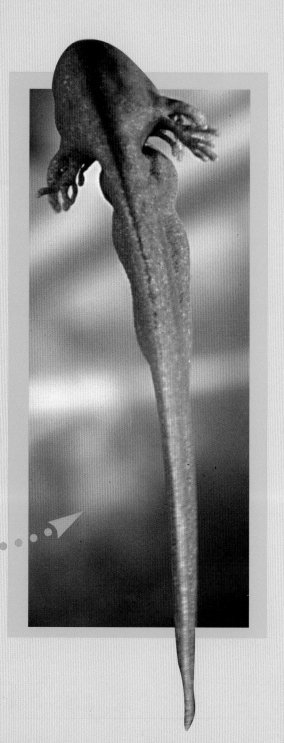

The tail makes the tadpole look like a little fish.

A frog cannot breathe underwater. A tadpole can. The tadpole has little slits called **gills**. The gills take in air from the water for the tadpole to breathe.

The tadpole eats her egg. Then, she eats water plants.

How does the tadpole change into a frog?

Growing Tadpoles

The tadpole grows bigger. Her body slowly starts to change. When she is about six weeks old, she grows two back legs.

The tadpole uses her back legs to swim faster.

Next, the tadpole grows **lungs**. She loses her **gills**. Now, the tadpole has to swim to the **surface** to breathe in air.

The tadpole uses her lungs to breathe in air.

Legs and Tails

About four weeks later, the tadpole grows two front legs. She now starts to look more like a frog.

*A tadpole's front legs grow through her **gills**.*

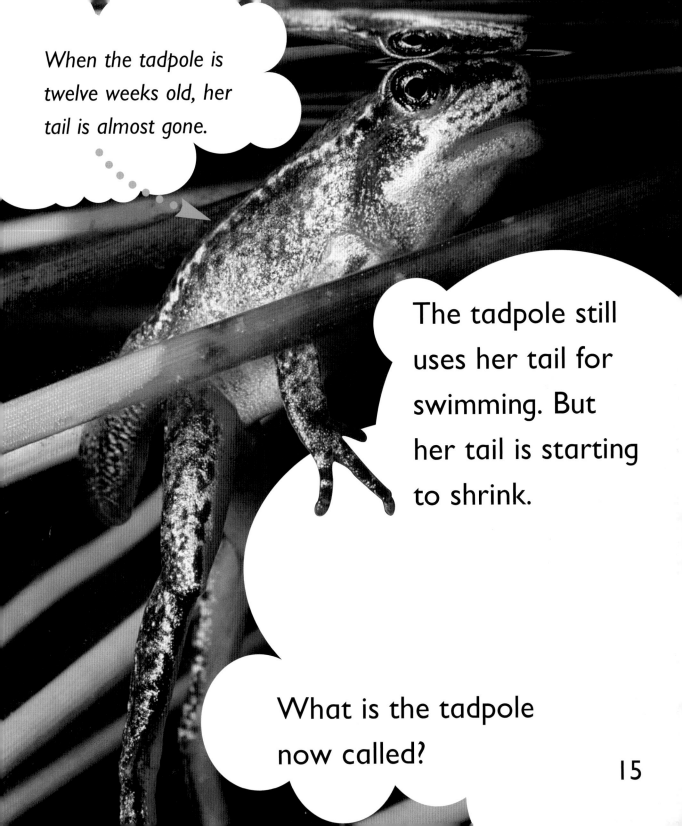

When the tadpole is twelve weeks old, her tail is almost gone.

The tadpole still uses her tail for swimming. But her tail is starting to shrink.

What is the tadpole now called?

15

Froglets

The tadpole now looks like a little frog. She is called a **froglet**. Her tail is now gone.

She uses her back legs and feet for swimming.

The froglet starts to spend time out of the pond. She climbs onto a leaf or a plant by the water.

When does the froglet leave the pond?

17

Life on Land

The **froglet** is about four months old. She leaves the pond. But she stays close to the water.

She hides among the long grass and stones.

She dives in to get her skin wet.

The froglet has to keep her skin damp.
Her skin cannot dry out. She needs to stay
close to the water to keep moist.

When is the
froglet grown up?

19

Hungry Frog

It takes the **froglet** about a year to grow up. Now, she is called a frog. The frog eats **insects**. She catches them with her long, sticky tongue.

Animals such as birds, bats, and grass snakes eat frogs. When the frog is in danger, she dives back into the pond.

This frog is in danger from a snake.

Where do frogs live?

Frogs at Home

Adult frogs live in damp places on land. They live in gardens, meadows, and woods.

*Frogs go back to the pond to **breed**.*

A frog can live for about eight years if it does not get eaten.

Frogs often hide during the day. They hide from animals that might eat them. Frogs come out at night to look for food.

Where does the frog go during the winter?

Winter Sleep

In the winter, it is cold. There is not much to eat. The frog goes into a deep sleep. This sleep is called **hibernation**.

The frog goes to sleep under a pile of leaves, moss, or stones.

During the winter, the frog's body slows down to save energy. She wakes up in the spring, when the weather is warmer.

Where does the frog meet a **mate**?

Meeting a Mate

The frog is three years old. She is ready to **mate**. In spring she goes to the pond where she was born. She finds a **male** frog to mate with.

*Male frogs make a low, croaking sound to call the **females**.*

When the frog has mated, she lays lots of eggs in the pond. Soon tadpoles will **hatch** from the eggs. The frog's life cycle starts again.

Life Cycle of a Frog

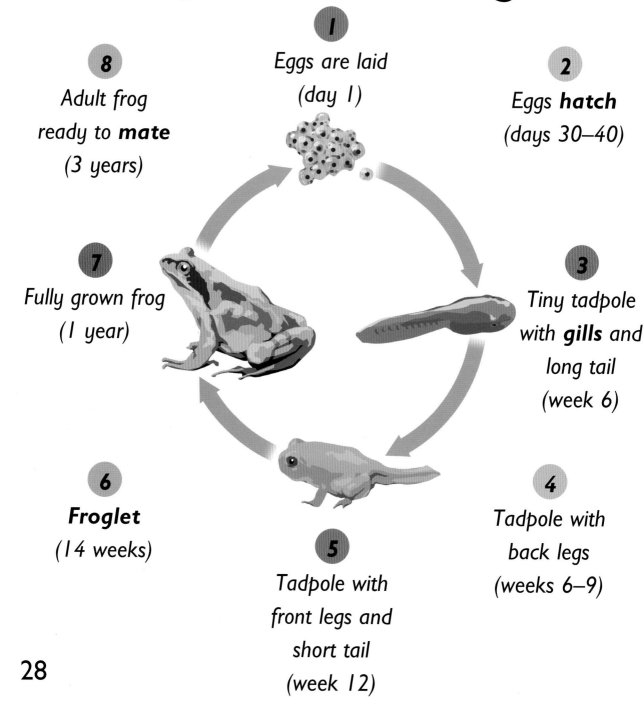

1
Eggs are laid
(day 1)

2
Eggs **hatch**
(days 30–40)

3
Tiny tadpole
with **gills** and
long tail
(week 6)

4
Tadpole with
back legs
(weeks 6–9)

5
Tadpole with
front legs and
short tail
(week 12)

6
Froglet
(14 weeks)

7
Fully grown frog
(1 year)

8
Adult frog
ready to **mate**
(3 years)

Tadpole and Frog

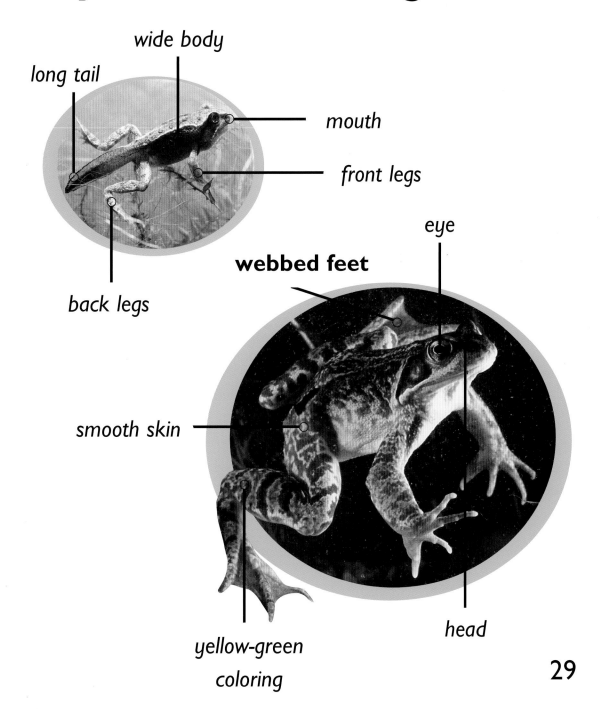

long tail

wide body

mouth

front legs

back legs

webbed feet

eye

smooth skin

yellow-green coloring

head

Glossary

amphibian animal that lives both in water and on land

breed to mate and have babies

clutch batch of frog eggs

female girl animal

froglet little frog

gills parts of an animal's body used to breathe underwater

hatch break out of an egg

hibernation long, deep sleep

insect small bug with six legs

lungs parts of an animal's body used to breathe in air

male boy animal

mate when a male and female come together to make babies. It can also mean the partner an animal chooses to have babies with.

surface top of the water

webbed feet feet with skin stretched between the toes

More Books to Read

Ganeri, Anita. *Nature's Patterns: Animal Life Cycles*. Chicago: Heinemann Library, 2005.

Parker, Victoria. *Life as a Frog*. Chicago: Raintree, 2004.

Royston, Angela. *Life Cycle of a Frog*. Chicago: Heinemann Library, 1998.

Saunders-Smith, Gail. *Frogs*. Mankato, Minn.: Pebble, 1997.

Spilsbury, Louise. *Life Cycles: Frog*. Chicago: Raintree, 2005.

Watts, Barrie. *Watch It Grow: Frog*. Mankato, Minn.: Smart Apple Media, 2003.

Index